MONSTERS HE MUMBLED

Dedicated to little monsters
everywhere

MONSTERS he mumbled

Written by sean o huigin
Illustrated by John Fraser and Scott Hughes

Black Moss Press

Monsters, He Mumbled was published by Black Moss Press
at 1939 Alsace Ave., Windsor, Ontario, Canada N8W 1M5.
Black Moss books are distributed in Canada and the U.S. by
Firefly Books, 250 Sparks Avenue, Willowdale, Ontario, Canada M2H 2S4
All orders should be directed there.

Black Moss Books are published in Canada with
the assistance of the Canada Council and the Ontario Arts Council.

ISBN 0-88753-187-3

Printed in Canada by
The National Press
Toronto, Ontario

TABLE OF CONTENTS

MONSTERS HE MUMBLED

monsters
he mumbled
they've taken
all my clothes

monsters
he mumbled
they've nibbled
off my
toes

monsters
he mumbled
they're driving
me insane

monsters
he mumbled
then he
hit me
with his
cane

monsters
he mumbled
because of
you they're
here

monsters
he mumbled
and bit me
on the ear

monsters
he mumbled
i'm getting
sick of
them

then he chewed
me up
for dinner
and he
spit me
out again
.

THE THING
AT TEACHEM WELL

there is a school
called
Teachem Well
where all
the students
behave well
there is
a reason for
that though
it is because
they had to
go if they
were bad
to see the
Gruk
a smelly thing
that lived
in muck
a puddle of
which can
be found
in the
children's
playing
ground

the teachers
went there
every day
to throw in
garbage
stuff which
they had
found within
the children's
pockets
toads and
worms and
smelly socks
that crawled
right off
the kiddies'
feet
smelling like
some rotting
meat

if once
a kid would
misbehave
it was sent
into the
waves the
Gruk
whipped up
when it was
hungry
so you see
the very young
they learned
quite quickly
to be good
or they
became
the old
Gruk's
food
their bones
got piled
on the banks
of that
deep pond

(the Gruk
burped "Thanks")

the teachers
would applaud
like mad
you see
it made them
very glad
to know the
Gruk
was on
their side
they knew
they never
had to hide
the creature
wouldn't eat
a teacher
they're too
tough
that's why they
beat you

it keeps their
muscles rough
and stringy
but kids
are fat
and plump
and springy

one day a
little girl
named Terry
sweet and
kind and
always merry
spilled some
paint upon
her desk
her teacher
screamed
"Why what
a mess!!!
You're doomed
you horrid
little child!"

poor Terry cried
the teacher
smiled
and dragged her
to the
Gruk's
pond edge
and there
out from
behind a hedge
another teacher
did appear
carrying an old
dead deer
with tire tracks
upon its
back
he threw it in
Gruk
threw it back
"I'm tired of
your bones and
meat!
I'm fed up with
those smelly
feet!

How would you
like to live
in muck
and have to
chew old
hockey pucks?"
he grabbed
the teachers
by their toes
and pulled
them in
up to the nose
he put young
Terry on
his shoulder
and as they
grew a little
bolder
they went into
the school
together
put all the
teachers
on a tether
dragged them
to the mucky
pool

you see the
Gruk
was no one's
fool
so now the
Gruk
is principal
and all
the kids at
Teachem Well
study harder
than before
and always
get
the highest
score
.

8

MY MONSTER

a
creature lives
beneath my
floor
it likes to
moan and scratch
and snore
it has a bump
upon its head
that's sometimes
green and
sometimes red

its nose is
running all the
time with
orange and purple
smelly slime
it loves to burp
and make strange
stinks
it sometimes
oozes up my sinks
and grabs the
soap from out
my hand
and then it laughs
to beat the band
but not a gentle
giggle

no
and not a jolly
Ho Ho Ho
its laugh is
like a dentist's
drill
it's high and
mean and
very shrill

some nights when
i am in my bed
i'll see its warty
drippy head
come peeking in
around my door

it almost seems to
sort of pour
its mushy body
where it goes
it has no feet
it just has
toes
all black and hairy
mostly nails
i even think it
has three tails
all full of scabs
and giant fleas

while hanging down
around its knees
are folds of skin
all grey and blue
it really likes
to slobber too
great greasy gobs
of yellow stuff
and if you think
that's not enough
its fingernails
are black and blue
from poking little
kids like you

it drags them in
from off the street
i've often seen
their little feet
disappearing
down its throat
and once it even
ate a goat
(it used the horns
for ice cream cones)
and when it's done
it spits the bones
upon my floor
and i'm fed up
with finding ears
in my tea cup
(it doesn't seem
to like that part)

so i will tell you
if you're smart
you won't come calling
at my house or
you'll be eaten
by that louse
that beast
that monster
that foul creature
i'd really hate
to see it
eat you
.

SMARTLAND

at Smartland School
i have been
told
there lives a thing
that's very
old
they found it when
they dug the
hole
where they would
build
that lovely school

they dug it up
with big
machines
it frightened
them
it let out
screams
that made the
workers'
hair turn white
they dream about
it every
night

its hair
is long
its face is
gooey
it ate a worker
they called
Louie
it schlurped him
up and then it
belched
and deep inside
poor Louie
yelped

the thing now
dwells between
the walls
at night it
crawls all
through the halls
of Smartland School
its ancient
place
the home of its
ancestral
race

the teachers
make the
children now
write monster
tales
and they tell
how poor Mary
disappeared
one day
as she was
going out
to play
she skipped
around a corner
gaily
and ran into
the thing
all naily
old and
wrinkled
getting fat
it glomped
her up as
quick as that

when Mary's
mother
came to shout
the principal
yelled
"OH WATCH OUT!"
alas too late
the beast had
got her
she soon joined
her lovely
daughter
deep inside
the ancient
belly
there with Louie
(he's still yelly)

the principal
ran out the door
and never was
seen anymore
the children now
all walk with
care
they know it
might be
anywhere

they never ask
to leave the
room
it could be
lurking
in the gloom
of
storerooms
restrooms
auditorium
the police chief
says they're
really boring
him
with their tales
of such a
thing
their stories
have a
phony ring
he's often come
to see the
place
he's never found
an ancient face
that peers at
him
or slobbers
badly

so you see
it seems
quite sadly
that the kids
of Smartland School
will make a
lunch
will make it
drool

the monster dug
up from the
ground
the awfullest
thing they've
ever found
when building for
an education
for the children
of our
nation
.

WALK MAN

there i was
walking down
the street
just swinging
along
listening to
the music
when suddenly
i felt these
long fingery type
of things
growing into
my earholes
and the
wires from
my headphones
started getting
thicker
and longer
and wrapping
themselves
around my body

and where the
tape recorder
was hooked
onto my
belt i felt
some kind
of rootlike
things
growing into
my waist

and then
i looked
into a store
window and
saw this
strange
robot sort of
creature
staring back
at me

well

that was
almost a year
ago and
about three
months later
i met this
really nice
girl thing
with kind of
tv sets for
eyes
and we got
married
and now
live happily
in our big
cardboard
box with our
two kids
Boob and
Tube
!

HEY YOU

i told you
to stop it

what's the
matter
are you
deaf
?

look at those
ears
my heavens
you haven't
polished them
for ages

look at them
their scales
are all dull
and lifeless

and look at
your nose
why isn't it
running

and when was
the last time
your sharpened
your teeth

what a disgrace

we can't take
you anywhere

creatures will
laugh at us
and throw
pudding

what have we
done to
deserve a little
creep like
you

what do you
think you
are

human
?

BEWITCHED

at Painsfield
school
one winter's
day
a strange thing
happened
so they say
a little kid
was seen
to fly
a hundred
feet
up in the
sky
it shot
out from
a top floor
window
it left
behind
its human
skin though
they found
it lying on
the floor

they hung it
up behind
the door
the child
landed on
the ground
the teachers
looked
and then
they found
their little
student
had been
changed
they saw
it now was
very strange
with fish
scales
where its
skin
had been
and from
its head
stuck up
a fin

something like
that on
a shark
instead of
hair
were leaves
and bark
the kiddy's
arms were
stretched out
long
there certainly
was
something
wrong

it looked up
at the
principal
and then it
burped
the poor man
fell
he never would
get any
older then out

there popped
from that
child's
shoulder
another head
all pink and
blue
i think it
looked
a lot like
you
don't go
to Painsfield
if you're
smart
the teachers
practise
in the
dark
so many ways
to change
their students
to things
resembling
snakes and
rodents

they're really
witches
in disguise

i say
don't go
there
if you're
wise
.

MONSTERS IN THE MORNING

how would
you like it?

just think
about it

holy cow
what a mess

everyday
it's the
same old
thing

i get up
i go to
brush my
teeth
i pick up
the toothpaste
i squeeze
the tube
and
out of
the tube
oozes a slimy
grey
worm
blinking its
eyes and
stretching
its body
('cause it

doesn't have
arms)
and yawning
at me

UUUUGGGGGGHHHHHHH!

so much for
my teeth

then
i go to have
a shower
and when i
turn on
the water
out of the
nozzle come
these long
skinny
green snakes
with icy
cold skin
and purple little
eyes
and they wrap
themselves
all around me
and start
licking me
with their
scratchy
tongues
and hissing
and whispering

and

I HATE IT
I HATE IT
I HATE IT

so i go
downstairs
to have
breakfast
and
when i open
the bread
all this
fuzzy orange
black stuff
comes crawling
out of
the bag and
curls around
my hand
and kind of
purrs
and the
jam jar pops
open and
this big mass
of gooey red
seedy stuff
bubbles out

so i go
back to bed
and crawl into
the sheets
but they've
turned into
this slippery
wet
plasticky
stuff
and they
tighten
around me
then sort of
shoot me
through the
window

so
here i am
at school
all messy
and smelly
and getting
yelled at
and it just
ISN'T FAIR
!

THE DINNER PARTY

the party was
a great success
the guests made
every kind of
mess
they dribbled
stew
they drooled
ice cream
they spit out
bones
and let out
screams

the food was of
the grandest sort
the kind that
didn't need
a fork

the meal began
with bits of
skin
the type you'd
find
a rat within
it wasn't cooked
oh heavens
no

its rawness made
your whiskers
grow

the next entrée
was made of
nails
finger
toe
all mixed with
snails whose

bodies had
been mushed
and crushed
the ladies present
really blushed
to taste its
flavour
somewhat like
a nightmare on
a moonless
night

the soup was
made of
things alive
with eyes that
opened very
wide the moment
that you took
a sip
and then
they'd bite
you on the lip

the main course
came on plates
of grass
with worms wove in
to give
them class

great slabs of
old and mouldy
bread
oozing green and
brown and red
gigantic hunks
of dirty feet
whose smell was
not what you'd
call sweet

all served with
apples full of
worms
the children
squealed and
jumped and
squirmed

dessert was made
from powdered
mouse
and cobwebs from
a haunted house
all mixed with
mud and gently
beaten
the nicest thing
you've ever
eaten

to end it
all they brought
out drinks
from dirty bathtubs
filthy sinks
with floating bits
of hairy soap
that tickled going
down your throat

so that was it
the feast of THINGS
who all flew home
on rubbery wings
to sleep and
dream of meals to
come
and listen to their
rumbling tum
.

ATMOSFEAR

don't go to
antarctica
don't go near
the ice
there's something
in there lurking
something not so
nice

beneath the drifts
of glittering snow
lies something evil
something low
something with long
icy teeth
something curled up
underneath the
ancient glaciers'
mighty cliffs
with blue cold steely
snarling lips

for centuries
it's lain there
trapped inside
its icy lair
listening as
each year goes
past to the
winter's icy
blast
but bit by bit
and drop by drop
as humans make the
air grow hot
pumping garbage
and pollution
they give to it a
neat solution to its
problem of
entrapment
it grinds its jaws
it tries to snap
them

it feels the
ice cap getting
thinner
as the atmosphere
gets grimmer
slowly
daily
drip by drip
it can feel
its prison
slip
turn to water
run away
just a little
every day
but the beast
is old as time
it's in no
rush
it doesn't
whine

someday when the
time has come
we'll hear a
roar
a thunderous drum
come rolling
through our
greying skies
as giant wings
and glaring eyes
rise up from the
earth's south end
we'll see the
icy creature bend
to peer upon our
tiny faces
we will find there
are no places
to escape its
viscious beak
or the claws
upon its feet

take warning now
this is no joke
we're doomed by
all the dust and
smoke we pour into
the air each day
we've got to find
another way
a kinder way to
treat the world
for deep inside
the ice is curled
this bringer of
a nasty fate
and who's to say
it has no mate
a dozen
two
or even five
trapped and waiting
but alive
waiting for we foolish
men to bring about
our own sad end
.